POEMS and PHOTOGRAPHY
by MRS. SIKAND

Printed and bound in the United States.

ISBN 978-0-910671-15-6

Library of Congress Cataloging-in-Publication Data

Joan Sikand

Title: Mind - A Sacred Place (poetry and photographs by Mrs. Joan Sikand)

Description: First edition - Path Press, Inc. Inc. 2016.

Identifiers: ISBN 978-0-910671-15-6 (alk. paper)
1. Religious poetry, American. 2. Spirituality--Poetry.
Classification: LCC PS3619.I478 A6 2016 | DDC 811/.6--dc23

LC record available at: https://leen.loc.gov/2016040697
LCCN 2016040679

Design and layout by 360 Nile Media, Kenya.

Publisher - Path Press, Inc., P.O. Box 5683, Evanston, IL 60204
E-mail - pathpressinc@aol.com

MIND -
A SACRED PLACE

POEMS and PHOTOGRAPHY
by MRS. SIKAND

Contents

DEDICATED TO OUR
SACRED HOLY FATHER,
WHO DWELLS IN EACH AND ALL OF US

INTRODUCTION

Poetry seems not to be obvious. 'Mind - A Sacred Place' is
universal. The writing of 'Mind - A Sacred Place', as is of 'Mrs.
Sikand', is that all humanity is interconnected in one whole, be it
'God' 'Allah' 'Krishna' 'Jesus' 'Buddha' 'Mother Nature'. 'Mind - A
Sacred Place' is about that interplay, the focus being on 'places'.
In my life, I have encountered so many people running around
searching for peace; flying to London, Paris, backpacking in the
Himalayas, California, New York, Kenya, etc. Peace is within. God
is within. It's about harnessing your mind to discover this one
reality, that all is within yourself. This is an important truth which
is lost today in this vulgar, repulsive age of gross materialism. We
cannot stop engorging ourselves with more and more consumption.
Kentucky Fried Chicken just opened 8 franchises in Nairobi, financing
an aggressive marketing campaign. This is a poor country, with
established culture. The local diet of beans, corn, greens, goat, is
good and healthy.

Obesity and high blood pressure are raging.

Extinction of our biodiversity is imminent.

Humanity urgently needs to come back to oneness with God.

We are destroying ourselves immeasurable and irrevocably. Our
track record is poor. So many broken lives, so much garbage, so
much wasted time chasing after nothing. The task of restoring is
beyond belief. Our statistics on crime and mental health are so
depressing. We are suffering a lot of pain. Our current, hyper-modern
culture incites fantastic hatred, betrayal, anger, rage, stress. This
in turn, is creating huge divorce, disease, misery, death. Although
I study, I cannot find any age which can match our current time
of nihilistic and fatalistic attachment. We are destroying ourselves
with greed and stupidity. The constant, escalating pollution and
degradation is of the planet, mind, body and spirit. Ours is an age of
unprecedented moral and ethical dysfunction and degeneration. The
human condition is collapsing urgently.

Throughout time, God has manifested himself through religions;
Christianity, Judaism, Buddhism, Hinduism, Islam. The church,
synagogue, mosque, temple, are places were these religions brought
together communities to pray and worship and study scripture; Bible,

Torah, Baghvad Gita, Sutras, Quran. Their beauty and grandeur are astonishing. Why were they built? At what cost? People created them with architects, stone, wood, glass, metals, great love and joy. Their purpose was to restore man's relationship with a higher knowledge to renew trust, belief, love and forgiveness in brotherhood. Intrinsically, God's purest manifestation is nature; earth, wind, sky, forest, rivers, oceans, creatures, etc.

'Mind - A Sacred Place' brings together many diverse images with poetry depicting a range of humanity, evolving and occurring. It can serve as a lens through which to see ourselves. Many people are coming to Buddhism today. Like Buddhist teachings, 'Mind - A Sacred Place' allows one to experience God in a moment. There is no need to search, wait, pine, suffer. Control is here and now, if only we open our eyes to witness that the only reality is non-reality and to cease our addicting, dangerous and suicidal attachments. Great peace is within a moment.

Poetry is about time; you don't need a lot of time to read poetry. A few minutes a day brings you cover to cover, and then you can start again. Each reading can be fresh. Poetry need not restrict nor judge. It is about experience. Humanity today needs to come away from emotion and examine experience dispassionately, to be critical. Non-attached. Healing can occur when we start. From healing, then comes freedom. Then comes peace, joy and love. Understanding. We can then live for our purpose, to know God through humility, service and a total commitment of our being, and renew ourselves with integrity and confidence.

Mrs. Sikand
Nairobi, Kenya.
May 2016.

Found

I found them.
There.
They were in my backyard.
The scriptures, I mean.
They have always been
there,
beside me.
Real.
Perfect.
Non-existent.
Non-material.

The fish seemed ok in the
aquarium.
Just swimming along.
Being.
Thought is relative to who
you are.
What you are.
The Taj Mahal;
A prison or a palace.
Mama Bertha in Harlem.
9 kids in Kibera.
You and me.

Working

Buying your poetry.
Asking for your signature.
Impressed.
Getting America to work.
Helping democracy.
Taking care of my Self.
Understanding my gender.
My time and space.
My here and now.
Waiting patiently for direction.
Coming.
I've been around long enough
now to truly believe in miracles.
The wonderful inner eye.
Blue. White. Gold.
God in me.

HELP

Help me.
I am drowning in contempt, cynicism,
    insane self-absorption, cruelty, meanness.
Drawn into chaos, anarchy.
Color-coded pre-kindergarten shit fascination.
Shocking poverty of maturity.
I am in pain.
I am suffering.
I am crying, weeping.
Diving into stupidity, callous indifference,
        ignorance, rage.
Sobering hymns.
Songs of praise.
Holy. Holy. Holy.

Praise God who is the King.
Who was and is, and is to come.
Forgiveness as a crown.
Fear not; I am always with you.
When you walk through the fire,
    You will not burn.
When you walk through the water,
I will lead.
Rivers cannot overwhelm.

Poetry my journey.
Not the goal.
Not the object.
Inspiration. Hope.
Restore. Pause. Meditate.

Brave

When recollection remembers even me,
    May I not be afraid;
May I be brave to soldier on.
Which amusements left at Coney Island?
Retreat? Refuge? Relief?
None but me.

Who can recognize the Lord?
You and me.
Here and now.
The good priest to study scripture.
To offer lessons.
To lead.
Eternal Father.
Maker and Master of all Heaven and Earth.
Screaming hallejujah.
Chanting amen.

Tears. Joy. Bliss. Release.

My God incarnation.
Truth alive and well.
Beauty within.
Prayer.   Worship.   Praise.
Serving Him always.
Patience.   Humility.   Trust.   Belief.
Supernatural powers come over me.
Happiness.   Joy.   Bliss.   Miracles and magic.
Strange and spectacular love.
Time can continue gladly and freely.
No stress; worry; grief; guilt; shame.

Hurricane

Hurricane coming.
Storm. Danger. Harm.
Where is my home?
Rest? Shelter? Comfort? Refuge?
No where to hide.
No where to run.
The game is over.
I am here and now.
Answer me.
Face me.
What have you done?
Where are you going?
How so lost?

After, in the park, a brilliant blue-jay flew
    between the sun soaked oak and maple branches.
The common brown sparrows were glad.

ALEX

The beautiful lady
    held the young man's hand.
She kissed him quietly,
    with great love.
Tears, weeping.
He was going off to war.
To fight for democracy;
    America.
For target, shoes, stores, candy bars, pizza, hamburgers,
    frenchfries.
You and me.
How much more beautiful can you be?
How great your thought?
How rich your mind?
How sure your step?
I was with my mother and the time of my birth;
    and, she loves me still.
Fragile. Simple. Pure.
How rare is this thing called;
Love.

Keeping pace with my indian
    brother and sister.
Returning to my original,
    indigenous way.
Nature. Sky. Water.
Allowing the Earth to heal.
Forgiving her her lack.
Abating, reigning desire.
Controlling negativity; harm; lust; greed;
    sin; wrong.

When the soil is right,
    a flower can bloom.

GROWING

Diving into our misery.
Our continued attachment.
Creating endless loss; karma.
Stop. Pause. Think. Reflect.
Meditate.
Consider your possibilities.
Time.
Have we forgotten from where we came from?
Where to go?
How to follow?
Who?
Me and you.
All of us together.
Bonded, secure.
Brotherhood.
Sisterhood.
Parenthood.
Neighborhood.
Livelihood.
Here and now.
Always.
Seventies jewish sex love.
Getting fucked.
Duped. Doped. Fooled. Confused.
Forgetting my origin.
Wallowing in sin.
Lust. Fornication.
How can I grow up?

How can I win?
God is in your heart.
He is in your mind.
Everywhere, together.
His Way to guide you
  Is the perfect way.
The only way.
Make no exceptions.
Staying on track,
     We can arrive at peace and love; direction;
     Purpose; trust; truth.

Anger and entitlement.
Pride and ego,
     Consume us like a raging fire.
Confidence kills.
Sex sells.
True love brief.
Death a moment.
Give me a miracle.
I can't hold on any longer.

CHARLIE

My urban temple.
My mental grove.
Blossoming. Occurring. Awakening.
Time passing effortlessly.
I am free.
Here and now.
Always near.
Never far.
By my side.
Nicely tucked away.
I can never fear.
I'll be okay.

Gray parrots in Machakos forest.
Chirping away.
Leaving seeds.
Which turn to plants.
Which bear fruit;
Figs and flowers.
Which monkeys eat;
    Sykes, vervets, colobus.
Rains passing.
Clouds billowing.
We are only human.
Pain. Sex. Love. Birth. Death.
Tomorrow.

After the gentle old lady
    passed away on Main Street,
        her photos remained to tell her story.
Country; war; immigration; family;
church; survival; revival.

Indeed, Charlie Brown knew
    which tree to pick for the Christmas pageant:
The one most humble, sincere, kind,
  beautiful, simple, honest, pure.

17

'M'

Schoolchildren at restaurants 7pm, Tuesday.
Mommy on her cell,
    closing deadlines; mapping tomorrow's meetings;
    setting up a conference call to London.
Where was the chocolate milk?
Shit about homework.
Oh, I HATE mom!
Older and wiser.
Learning and growing.
Time moving.
Standing tall.
Changing.
Given a second chance.
We are free.

Selling smoking paraphernalia and
    cheap rock CD's on 86th St.
Mike thought about his college days.
What a fucking waste of time.
Degree. Marriage. Kids. Job. Divorce.
    Loss.
What a mess.
Thank god for marijuana.
He couldn't afford the painkillers,
    and getting high helped.
When your mind sloughs off,
    It really is a challenge.
Beauty was everywhere.
Rich and poor alike.
All was one and absolute.
Ok. It works.
America within myself.
To comprehend that I am that change; the object;
    The goal.
Not waiting.

Not whining, inert, ashamed.
To honor and respect.
Meditating on the overwhelming power of God.
Practicing His Ways.
Holy Light.
Graceful, fruitful, easy.
Finally, he was ok.

Her son, Michael, came home from
 his first day at college.
He brought home a book on Korean history
 inscribed by the Dr., Rev. John Y. Paik,
 her old pastor.
How wonderful!
How strange!
How miraculous!
How much she had loved church service.
Reciting the Apostle's Creed.

Mikey, aged 7, a Chinese boy was doing
 his homework in a Flushing downtown restaurant.
His parents were busy serving noodles.
Pork. Beef. Chicken. Seafood. Tofu.
His favorite was pork.
'M' was his favorite letter.
He wrote tall, pointy 'M's,
 and short mushroomy ones.
Pages and pages.
It looked like mountains.
He had not forgotten.
He remembered.
He was, ok.

Rohtang Pass

I write this because I love you.
Because, I care.

Sexual awakening creates a myriad
    of consequences.
A heaven or a curse.
Unwanted children.
Hatred. Confusion. Lust. Greed.
Love.
The possibilities are endless.
And, so they are.
Temple. Mosque. City.
Walking and falling on the ground.
Losing your balance to create injury.

Climbing Rohtang Pass to pray.
The Dalai Lama waiting.
Baby on the back, wrapped in a Kullu shawl.
A boy.
Blue. White. Red. Green. Yellow.

The corporate executive
    walked into the boardroom.
Her high heels clicking on the black granite floor.
Her two young children were at home
    with the nanny, piercing long, sharp pins
    into the eyes of their dolls.
Her eyes glowered, narrowed;
    Her red lips pursed.
Sell, she hissed, at any price.

Danghar Monastery, July.
Waking at 3am.
Stars. Night sky.
Water. Big job.
Yoga. Surya namaskar.

Dressing.
Washing. Walking outside.
Falling.
Bleeding.
Cleaning.
Healing.
Sun rising.
The cool of the Himalaya.
Gushing forth.
Giving life.
Again.
Wavering between doubt and fear.
Control, despair.

Staying still and watching the world
    change around you.
Rising sun.
Breeze.
Clouds.
Air.
Dust.
Light.
Mountain.
Temple.
Mind.
My perfect room.
Facing temple and mountain together.
Windows all around.
Toilet nearby.
Knowing one's mind is the only success.
Choosing God's way.
Peace. Love. Forgiveness.
Praising His Name.
Hare Krishna. Hare Ram.
Contemplating His Image.
Prostrate. Kneeling.   Bowed.
Following His Path.

Silence. Quiet. Meditation.

A father who loves his daughter with all his
    heart.

A mother completely devoted to her son.

No more defilement.

Ruin. Loss. Pain.

Children who please their parents.

A happy marriage.

Contentment. Time. Peace.

To be a great mind
    One must experience pain;

You need to comprehend only the
    frailty of man against the magnitude of
    God.

Then, you are great.

You are one.

You achieve skill.

Awareness. Intuition. Knowledge.

Control.

The signs of God are manifold;

Illustrious, good.

Cross. Book. Candle. Bell.

It is you.

It is me.

We have arrived.

Descending and arising.

We are free.

WHISPER

What is in a whisper?
When I take stock of my life,
    What will be the gauge?
The measure, the time?
To recognize a miracle,
    to be immersed in this true knowledge
    is called grace.
To love life
    you need to control the senses.
Careful thought.
Right mind.
Good action.
No fear.
Cool head.

Shaping things for my sole benefit,
So that I can consume more and more.
Never a surfeit.
Pure gluttony, passion, defeat.
Continue in my taking, polluting,
    desecrating, fornicating, sin.
How real is grief? Sorrow?
 Despair? Depression?
What do I own, possess?
Of what value are they to me now?
They have no matter.
No meaning.
No cost.
Carefully guarded by my fantasies.
Controlled by my limits.
Time. Decay.
I will be okay.
What about eating?
Shit and crap.
Terrible stuff.

Demonic, barbaric ways.
What about oil?
Who cares?
What about shopping?
Waste and garbage.
Dragging our feet through
    this ragged, wretched race.
Afraid to fall.
To get off.
Change.
Believe.
Behave.
Have faith –
    In God.
Ourselves.

Lady

At what point do we paint a portrait of our Lady?
At what point of sickening disbelief?
Scorn. Forlorn. Torn. Born.
Anew. Afresh. Restored.
Staying inside to hear the rain.
To listen.
Be quiet.
Take time.
Rest.   Meditate.
In the far Northeast, there is an empty temple.
Her lost high priestess wandering, forgotten, waiting for
return, release.

The poor woman lay on her back, exhausted.
Tears streaming slowly down her face.
After all that.
Another daughter.
Yet another girl.
How could she face her husband?
Four daughters.
They needed a son; badly.
A boy to carry things on.
The land was tough.
Seasons brutal.
Without a son, everything would collapse.
Yes; she was worried.

Guan Yin's feet hurt.
Try on so many shoes;
She only got so far as leather sandals;
Made for Jesus, Buddha, Mohammed, Allah, Christ, Emmanuel,
Moses, Abraham, Joseph, Krishna, Ram.
Otherwise, her feet would always pain.

Children playing in the sun.
Laughing, running, happy.
In Joy and Peace.

AMINA

Amina on the swings at Kissena Park.
Her head scarf flying in the chilly breeze.
Pink, with splashes of green and brown.
At seventeen, she could be pretty.
Memories of her tragic, war torn country
floating, whirling, cascading in her mind.
She kept swinging.
Flood. Poverty. Guns. Chaos. Evacuation.
She was getting very tall, and chubby.
Her parents worried; a lot.
The Koran exhorted that in all things,
Allah reigned in goodness, mercy, kindness, fruit.
But, quite frankly, cracks were emerging.
Doubts were creeping in.
Yusuf and his wife suffered greatly.
Tariq had cancer.
The rent was long overdue.
The weather was freezing.
Ice and snow.
Al Jazeera smoked.
Fires were burning.

Amina walked in;
Fresh as spring.
The cedars and cherries returned.
Alive.

White Scarf

Do you feel like screaming?
Crying?
Dying?
Living?
Surviving?
Seeing?
Seeing what?
The Earth being destroyed so
Passionately?
Unrelentlessly?
Barbarically?
Brutally?
Savagely?
Let's move on .

Psycho shit.
Mass decay.
Filth.
Loss. Pain.

A young African girl walking barefoot
     in the hot sun;
        Wearing a white scarf.
Ignoring the pain.
Fetching water,
     in the burning sun.

Totality of God.
One with his way.
Birth. Death. Time.

Friends never benefit.
Foes cannot harm.

Saint

Spiritual concentration is
    eventually called Meditation.
To seek such things is good, correct,
    pure, nice.
Try it; and attain
    everlasting peace, tranquility, love.
The death of my master.
Saint reborn.
Om Shanti.
Om Jesus Christ.
Om Hari Krishna.
Om Namah Shivayah.
Om Bismallah.
Om Ali Akbhar.

Man

I want to be the master of my ideas.
I want to control my senses;
    my Mind.
See clearly.
Think wisely.
Move quickly, with:
    Health;
    Speed;
    Love;
    Devotion;
    Brotherhood;
    Man.
These possibilities are good.
I want these ones.
    The ones of:
    Godliness;
    Holiness;
    Righteousness;
    Peace.
What is your plan?
What is your way?
I want to go.
I obey.

CHRISTMAS 2012

Lord, make me an instrument of your peace.
Where there is hatred let your love increase.
Let compassion and mercy
    follow me all the days of my life,
    and I will dwell in the
    House of the Lord forever.
His Way a lamp unto my feet.
A guide. A beacon. A light.
No fear.
Humility. Gratitude. Love. Forgiveness.
Time. Healing. Beauty.

The stars and quarter-moon shining on an
    African Christmas night.
Moonlight antelope nibbling on dry brittle grass.
The predictions are dire.
The times dark, demonic, indeed.
Death, despair, grief.
A black scarab 4 inches long on its backside.
Legs in the air, wiggling.
Determined to right itself.
The struggle done.
Work begun.
Forward marching.
Continuing along.

They say the endtime is near.
Where will you be?
Mind balanced?
Clear?

H❂art

Rev. Helen Kim looked out at her church congregation.
The usual four had arrived on time;
10:00 am Sunday.
Mrs. Morris, Mr. Kim, Kathy Klark, Jim.
Just four, but they truly loved her.
There was a magnificent bouquet of tiger lilies, wild orchids,
    roses, surrounded with fern and palm, at her alter.
She spoke, to recall:

'Through endless ages the Mind has never changed.
It has not lived, or died, come or gone, gained or lost.
It isn't pure or tainted, good or bad, past or future, true
or false, male or female.
It isn't reserved for teachers or lay people.
Elders, or youth, masters or idiots, the enlightened or
the unenlightened.
It isn't bound by cause and effect and doesn't struggle
for liberation.
Like space, it has no form.
You can't own it and you can't lose it.
Mountains, rivers or walls cannot impede it.
But this Mind is ineffable and difficult to experience.
It is not the Mind or the senses.
So many are looking for this Mind,
Yet it already animates their bodies.
It is theirs, yet they don't realize it.'

Her beauty radiating, they all got up satisfied, at peace.

The Banker

'Do you believe your miracle has come?'
Said the Devil to the Banker.
'Yes, indeed. You have been my friend
    for so many years. Why not?'
The Devil smiled.

'Fine. Kindly sign your final contract.'
The Banker sprang to action.
'Which terms?'
'The diamonds', sneered He.
'They are now entirely yours.'
In the early twilight, sparkling gems
    twinkled merrily.
Greedily he signed.
'Thanks!'
By mid-morning, the Banker, in horror,
realized they were only dewdrops
    frozen briefly by the late-night hoar frost.
In the ambulance, before lunch, he died.

Common worship

Religion is a quality of energy,
    Our time, place, humanity.
Descending and arising.
Church, temple, mosque, square, city, slum.
Transcending spirit.
Yogic mind.
Consolation. Humility. Service.
Forgiveness. Love.

My Father's weddings.
Solemnizing marriage vows.
Thumb-eared Book of Common Worship.
Until death do us part.
Trust. Loyalty. Faithfulness. Unity.

GONE

We were feeling real bad
 that the house and its wondrous garden
 had been sold.
Thankfully, Jane thought to take pictures of the
 fated, majestic garden.
Sadly, she walked around and snapped:
 the giant 100 year old Ngumu tree;
 the oddly coloured rubber tree;
 the very tall fire-red bottle-brush tree.
The ancient, mighty palm.
Frangipani; massive jacaranda. Giant cactus.
The cacophony and riot of
 green, yellow, purple, pink, fuchsia, white.
Birds; swallows, weavers, kites, ibis.
A snake or two.
Now. Gone.
Massacred. Slaughtered. Humiliated. Killed.
Destroyed.
Gone.
Only ditch, mud and slime remained of
 that previous glory.

Cake

Aunty Abha's pineapple upside down cake.
The oven went off two times.
Anyway, ok.

I love to hear prayer.
Longing for God comes so easily.
Reaching for His Ways.
Being. Reading. Studying. Listening.
Singing. Dancing. Praising.

Will I have able children?
Will my parents be at peace?
Will my way be right?

I find I still love her.
I find I still care.

EKTAA

Her silence spoke a million words.
Her breath, a whisper.

We are all of us connected
    to a greater whole.
We are none of us apart.
Holding my memories.
Encased.
Enraptured of recollection, truth.
Elevate your mind,
    just a teeny, weeny bit.

Begin. Start. Go.
Commence. Graduate. Continue.
Again.
The persona of my dreams.
Diaphanous moon.
Orbit radiating.

Mass addictions.
Crazed, demented attachments.
Fixes; control; disease; grief;
fornication; cocaine; heroine; radiation; pot;
lust; greed; selfishness; gluttony; stupidity; jealousy;
    anger; guilt.
Do you laugh at me?
Or, do you cry?
Tears of sorrow, shame, remorse.

We are all from the same source.
We are none of us differentiated.
All are equal.
All are free.
No need to fear.
We are okay.
All possess: wisdom, choice, thought,
    action, grace, peace, forgiveness, calm, healing,
    light, love.
Our commonality is our strength,
    guide, way.
Ektaa.
Om so'ham

NOW

A moment of memory, peace.
Love.
Unbroken.
Pure.
Unadulterated.
Uncontaminated.
Unpolluted.
Fresh.
New.
The best my fruit can do,
    is enough.
No complaint.
No worry.
No fear.

CHRIST

I will pray for the
    Christ realization in you;
For, I am your:
    Prophet;
    Poet;
    Spirit;
    Muse.
Knowing right from wrong.
Consciousness, balance.
I am free.

SOUL MATES

Another realization.
Otra vez, milagro.
We are, in fact, soul mates.
Ok. I remember.
Our spirits were before;
Monkeys, rhinos, elephants, carrots, ostrich eggs, redwood
    trees, dogs, 2 orange cats with fluffy white collars and ever-
    changing eyes.
And, very often, king and queen in so many distant lands.
Ancient, timeless, forgotten days.
My favorite places were northern highlands facing west.
Cold, snow and wind. Alpine forests.
Hawks, eagles, tigers.
Om shanti. Hari Om.
Our people were tribal; nomadic.
We moved in tents and horses.
Luckily, as the king, you gave me a carriage.

What is a soul-mate?
True love incarnation.
Found. Perfect. Pure.
Without fault; no mistake.
Absolute. Ecstatic.
Free.
In you; in me.
Together.

TO BE

Carefully guarded secrets of myself.
Who I am.
Where I am.
What I can be.
From where I came.
To where I will go.
Following; sliding; sailing;
swimming.
Being.
Chanting prayers at my birth and death.
Holy light.
Spiritual gifts.
Transcendency.
Ascendency.
Descendency.
Alive.
What is the value of my worth?
The truth of my beginning?
My here and now?
Senses; breath.
Life.

CRAVING

Waiting for a miracle.

Insisting.

Tears of blood running down my
cheeks.

Rivers of hope and desparation.

Craving for the Divine.

The Impossible.

The Real.

It can be done.

It is here and now.

SEVENTIES

Psychedelic Woody Allen sex shit.
Martha Graham. Billy Graham. Ravi Shankar.
The Beatles. Vietnam. POW's.
Staying awake.
Church on Sundays.
Putting on your best.
Shining. Stellar. Restful. Pleasing.
Beautiful. Gorgeous.
Hot summer city.

The rain showering.
Running for your swim suit
to cool down.
Material electoral distortions.
Correct me if I'm wrong.
Please, kindly, do.
Love me.
Cold war.
FBI.
CIA.
Nixon.
KGB.

Container of my youth.
The shopping mall.

CAM

ITO

I

The mixture and time of
    Who I am.
Where I want to go.
From where I came.
Goals. Spirals. Descending.
Have you ever made mistakes?
The truth could kill us.
Destroy and shatter our beliefs, illusions, distortions.

When will fame ever find me?
To be recognized; popular – wise.
The time to heal is here and now.
Renewal ever-present; ever-sure.
It may hit us like a tornado; hurricane;
    monsoon; earthquake; tsunami.
A great tidal wave; massive act of God.
Great horrible acts of nature.
Our own terrible undoing.
All we have left at the end, can be our relationships.
Glory. Duty. Beast.
Let's all be recognized.
Counting ourselves.
Play the right game.
If we can define
    how we can use our way, and be decent,
    respectful – clean; we can be better.
Sunlight falling on ancient Venetian walls.
The Vatican approving.
All at peace. Restore. Calm. Impartial. Temperance.
Luck. Center. Control.

Where there is birth, there is hope.
Where love can restore itself in renewal;
    Yes, we can go on.
Tarry.

The fall season ensuing.
Green; brown; gold; shades lingering.
Filtering.
Continuing along.

Religion.   Don't lose it.
Don't abuse it.
It can work for some; but, not for others.
So what?
Leave it alone.
Let it go.
Let it be.
Ego; pride; practice.
All power of the: Christian; Prophet; Jew.

For a while the wicked man prospers;
    But then he withers like a weed;
    Like a grain of wheat that has been cut down.
Can any one deny that this is so?
Can any prove that this is untrue?
You learn to love God.
It finally sinks in.
You have arrived.
You have come home.
Time and place okay.
Right where you are.
God exists in every form; in every way; everywhere.
It occurs through prayer.
Through the worship of God.
The unwavering belief in miracles.
The magic of here and now.

It plays itself again.
Again, a child.
Again, today, tomorrow, yesterday.
Again, a memory, experience, conclusion.
Again, a smell, touch, time.
Another chance to win; or, fail.

Freedoms polluted and violated.

II

Early morning birdsong - in tune.
Joy. Harmony. Bliss.
Expressing from the heart true love and joy.
In total God being.
Writing my book.
Expressing thought.
Experience. Totality. Complete and utter unity,
    with God, myself, I.
Evangelistic nature – Guiding me.
Choosing me. Near to me. Never far.
How to pray? I need peace.
How to worship? I want to know God.
Invite Him to my house.
Allow Him entry to my Heart.
Give God control over my Being.
My every moment.
Awakening.
Hallejujah.
Praise.
Songs of joy.
Cries of great devotion.
Thirst for His Glorious Way.

Her heart bled for the broken, dying world.
Her eyes bulged in fear and terror of the
    disaster yet to come.
Misery. Failure. Destruction. Sorrow. Loss.
Deafening spiritual silence.

North Korean starvation.
A deep chill within my bones.
Blizzards howling.
Frozen, barren planet.

Barbie, Ken, Monopoly, Scrabble, Brady Bunch.
A taste for retail.
Forgetting the real.
Hunger. Loss. Fear. Falling. Flying.
Dying.
Free.
Spiritual guidance, protect me.
I am not afraid.
Facing evil.
The beast.
Lead the way.

Truth. Myself.
Arriving at supreme fantasy.
Stories of the good pastor.
The faithful shepherd.
God's house.
Temple. Door. Path. Way.
My family.
Providence.
Many servants to follow.
Build His house.
Raise His church.
Losing a treasured parent.
Finding your way; growing.

IV

Guan Yin, Jesus, Mohammed, Krishna, Buddha sat at dinner.
Guan Yin's feet were bare.   She wore no shoes.
A pale green veil hung over her gorgeous topknot.
Before her, on the table, was a lovely salad of green lettuce,
    avocado, sliced tomato in balsamic vinegar, virgin olive oil,
    sprinkled with sea salt, and freshly cracked black pepper.
Jesus wore a robe of burgundy and blue.
A crusty loaf of freshly baked bread and a silver goblet
    of rare deep red wine before him.
Mohammed, in turban and beard, had a nice
    piece of roast goat, with a yoghurt dipping sauce; some red chili.
Krishna wore a gold tunic, his neck jeweled with rubies, emeralds,
  sapphires.
Before him, spicy daal, roti, jeera palao, served on a banana leaf.
Buddha's right shoulder was exposed.
His bowl was empty.
Guan Yin spoke first,
"All is Mind. All is not Mind."
Jesus said, "I am the Truth and the Way.
No one shall come to the Father but by Me."
Mohammed, "Al hamdullilah"
Krishna, "Om namo baghavati, vasudevaya."
Buddha, remained speechless.

V

A slowing down of time.
An ebbing of sorrows.
Losing your mind.
An overdose of drugs.
Waiting; hoping; surviving; dying; dreaming; being.
Breathing a solitary air.
Quiet. At peace. Humble. Divine.
Fresh morning dew.
Cool sky.
Many birds flying above.
Great trees.
Massive, mighty forest.
Fresh, glorious, wonderful breeze.
Breathe of God.

Time of myself.
Free.
Offensive dirt and grime.
Constant toil and sweat.
Never-ending gnaw for more.
Never enough.
Always, always, always, always more.
Everyone given up.
Lost. Forgotten. Dead.
If you can't recognize grief,
How will you get better?
Change? Heal? Recover? Restore?
Grounded by my way.
A higher being.
Larger. Bigger. Better.
Me.
God.

God in me.
Always perfect.
Free.
I am going to let that grief guide me.
A small price to pay for peace of mind.
A general to lead my army.
Rank. Class. Time.
In joy there is no matter.
In bliss, happiness, no form.
No beginning; nor, end.
As for me and my house,
We will serve the lord.
My boast in you alone.

VI.

'Which elephant are you? The right or left?'
Smiling, she wiggled her gold and elephant hair earrings.
His gift.
Her husband laughed.
He really loved her.
He was especially thankful to God
    for His great blessing, that He had granted such immense
    love, warmth and understanding, joy, life, happiness.
Constantly they loved God.
Joyfully they gathered their lives together, and
    daily worshipped Him.
How? Always they loved each other.
Service, gratitude, caring, believing.
Intelligence. Smart. Handsome. Lovely. Loyal.
Funny. Fun. Ok. Trusting. Remembering. Sharing.
Patient. Forgiving. Kind. Generous. Honest. Faithful.
Warm-hearted. Big-hearted. Enjoyable. Delicious. Good.
Life will go on.
Continue. And, also hope.
Future, healing. Control.

This world gone amok, can, of course be saved.
Reborn. Restored. Renewed, afresh.
The power of our times can adorn us.
Betray us.
Become us.
Not me. Not I. No way.

Chanting Prajnaparamitasutra.
The joy of being alive.
The happiness of life.
Careful. Thoughtful. Wise.
You cannot stop the hands of time.
You cannot reverse the clock.
Living in God always.
Effortlessly. Forever. Again.
Love associations of warmth, sunshine, gratitude.
Seeking a harmony with nature.
Restoring mind.
Thirsting for God.
To master my attention.
To make me whole.
A syncretic, heroic life.
Obeisance. Joy. Sorrow.
Pleasure. Pain.
The miracle would come.
It was here.
The scream of his heart.
Pleading; waiting; urgently; for –
Man's awakening.
Quietly, silently – watching.

The way to fight danger is-
HEAD ON.

VII

Freedoms polluted and violated.
Duty. Breach. Failure. Injury.
Constitutional rights completely trampled.
A gesture of the hand.
The tort of gross parental negligence.

The last tzar of Russia running around Brooklyn;
Trying to find his way home.
Fantasy of my guilt, shame, death, loss.
Expressions of God overwhelm me.
Excite me.   Deceive me.
Intelligent man.
Written word.
Effervescent charm and passion.

Life is only a game of vain and senseless politics.
When all is said and done,
You will have only yourself to blame; to consider.

VIII

Grateful that her son practiced prayer.
That in this world of guns, drugs, hatred,
sickening violence, rage, he heard the word of God.
That he followed, at his age, the best he could;
Humility, obedience, intelligence, hope.
Not yet to face life's butchery.
Not yet tested.
Still, his mother meant to him, the most, for now.

IX

A painting herself.
The many colors of the rainbow;
Purple, brown, yellow, red, blue, green.
Her moods and swings adorned her.
A very uncommon person.
A rare bird indeed.
His love for her was unspeakable.
He could find no words to express his deep,
Profound emotion.
And, the great joy and miracle
was that this blessing was well understood.
They were both of them glad.
They enjoyed the quiet and trust of their love.
As such, it was truly a miracle.
God's grace had truly, really been born.
Every moment is a miracle.
Every breath, a dream.

The deep, heart-rending pain of losing the one
You cannot have.
Moving onto another chapter.
Time.   Place.   Experience.   Death.

The seed took a minute.
Glorious. Beautiful. Bliss. Ecstasy.
At least its physical.
Maybe I can bear it.
Danger avers me.
Risk averse.

A desperate world, in a desperate age.
We are starving for soul. Touch.
Raging contortions of self-defeat.
The immense prospect of disaster.

Watching and waiting.
Knowing righteousness will prevail –
God never far.
An exhausting read.
Coming back to my room.
Quiet.   Birds singing outside.
Some cars.
A cool early October breeze;
Giving me another day.

Las guerras grande.
Muchos muertos
Mucho dolor totalmente.

Seeking a harmony of nature.
Restoring mind.
Thirsting for God.
Dreading the empty sorrow and loneliness
if my mother should leave me.

Her lovers, fantasies, sexual awakening.
Tantric cave and serpent engorging.
Do I need to put some sex in the equation?

And, if so, then what?
The joining; the coupling.
The wonderful pleasure.
The strong abiding desire.
Done.
Cursing the very thing
Which is loved and treasured.
Killing the beast to avoid the beauty.
Alienation, discomfort, alone.
Living in a world crowded with loneliness.
The winter of my ideals.
The truancy and dormancy of ideas.

The good pastor had to file for a permit.
He really had to scream-
'FUCK YOU!'
But, the poor man had nowhere to go.
No one cared at all.
The guilt, sorrow, knowledge,
was only,
sadly, his own.

"The first shall be last; and the last shall be first."

XI

Continuing.   Gravity.
Tomorrow will come.
Doing what you can.
To get through life in just one piece.
I want a faith like that.
One that inspires.
What to do with all those old books?
Useless knowledge.
Faded vision.
Lost goals.
Broken ideals.
Forgotten soul.
Hypocrisy.   Lies.   Deceit.
You cannot correct society by
imprisonment and punishment.
This has never and will never be the case.
True change can only come from:
Peace; Brotherhood; Togetherness;   Thanksgiving.
Trust.
Religion – naturally, without constraint, pressure, stress.
Glorious spring.
Summer showers.
Chilly autumn.
Snow winter.
Again.
Eternal; never dying.
No end; no beginning.

I'm so glad that you love me.
Happy that you can't let me go.
Holding my hand, leaning on you;
I'm glad.

XII

Man living in nature.
Drinking dew.
Taking grass and animal.
Bare feet.   Long hair.   Nude.
No ego. No shame.   No pride
Living humbly before his maker.
Equal with the earth.
Caring for creation.
Wonder.   Awe.   Respect.
Rising temperatures.
Changing ways.
Solar eclipse over falling moon.
Asteroids.   Comets. Meteorites.
Disaster.   Doom.

Show me your face, o lord.
Shine your radiance upon me.
Lead me to follow you always.
I want to step in your shoes.
I want you to hold my hand.
Comfort me.   Guide me.   Love me.

To carry a child, your liver
    gets really crushed.   Wow!
A healthy mother can beget a healthy child.
Tough liver makes a tough baby;
    One who cries, struggles, gets along.
One who yet may stand, grow, walk, talk,
    See, think, feel, work, love, hate.
Be.
The liver supporting the back, her womb,
    her child, becoming one.
Prajnaparamita sutra.
Radiant wisdom of the ultimate.
Arriving at the magic of your presence.
I am touched.
Breathing; I live.
Aware of your embrace;
    Effulgent way.

XIII

Bobby Fisher. Kissinger. Idi Amin. The Cold War.
Hello Kitty. Cabbage Patch. Kellogg's Cornflakes.
Gomer Pyle. Frank Sinatra. Rev. Moon. Patty Hearse. Charles
Manson. Jimmy Carter. Boycotting grapes.

If I should ascend to the temple of my mind;
Bats. Toilets. Filth.
Stuff I cannot bear; cannot call my own.
A vow of poverty; silence; truth.
Beyond prayer, belief.
A recollection of time, voice, experience, thought.
Would you be a constant with me? Together?
Always in my life?
A smile on the verge of tears.
Who will make the rules?
Who can be in charge?
Lead? Guide? Follow? Share?
Compare?

Gambling debts galore.
Massive monster of deceit and lies.
Choking us, starving us.
Controlling. Annihilating.
You cannot change.
Time. History. Experience.
She sucked in her breath.
Closed her eyes, and had sex.
She made love.
Sensuality became her.
Indeed, she was beautiful,
   gorgeous, unique, nuts.
Changing your mind.
Taking your time.
Following, joining, togetherness, caring, love.
Know me.
Know God.
No more.   No less.
Always. Forever. Eternal.
I am.

XIV

Is a promise not enough?
Word unspoken.
Breath unbroken.
Senses. Mind. Thought. Way.
Kindness. Love. Understanding. Peace
Everlasting. Constant. Sure.
Life. Pleasure. Pain. Joy. Time. Experience.
Buying stuff for your kids.
Ever-expanding gain and girth.
Continuing, always.
Sweating. Dying. Lying.
Sighing. Declining. Wasting away.

To deliver children, only to
    mutilate them with hatred.
Crazy, fucking bitch.
Whore, creep, bastard, jerk, devil, demon, womb.
Adultery, fornication, rape, pollution, corruption, disease,
    misery, suffering, weeping, tears, death.
Me, myself, I.
My brother my enemy.
My sister cursing me.
My children destroying me.
My parents lost and forgotten.
Comfort me in this time of hell.
Demon raging gravity.

What the outcome will be,
No one knows.

No one dare consider.
Ruin, misery, death, loss.
Glad for the here and now.
Sad for these times.
A feverish, all-consuming love.
When I look in your eyes, I see me.
To capture time still.
Kings and queens and made up things.
Living a life of lies.
Deceiving yourselves.
Crapping upon ourselves.
Destroying ourselves.
A false mark of guilt, sin, experience.
Travelling along.
Carrying us to an unknown course.
Stars. Moon. Sun. Clouds. Rain.
Fate. Destiny. Tomorrow.
1,000,000 year old carbon.

XV

Sitting in a hotel,
      waiting for a meeting.
Selling industrial equipment at
      a conference in Africa.
Extraction industries.
Development. Progress.
Sign the contract.
Screw the deal.
Pump that shit.
Take it away.
Trade.
Are we polite?
Do we have manners?
Do we care?
All consuming greed.
Insanity.

XVI

A humble woman asking for God's light.
A sincere man seeking realization.
A little child hopeful, sure, convinced.
Vital, virile man.
Becoming, lovely woman.
My child has come home.
My son is here.
My daughter has just arrived.
I am with them.
Here and now.

Suicidal ways.
Darkened, blackened days.
Do it already.
What are you waiting for?
Screw me!
Shit. Rape. Fuck. Destroy. Rampage.
Evil. Carry on.
Still.
I can forgive you.
I can heal.
Certainly, we must carry a heavy load.
Tirelessly continue.
Endlessly travel.

XVII

Guidelines for positive parenting.
Living freely; truth; resolve.
A Lutheran church in Paterson, NJ.
Presbyterian, Anglican, Methodist, Baptist,
Seventh Day Adventist, Jehovah's Witness.
Great and ancient cathedrals – Notre Dame, St. Albans, St. Paul's,
St. John the Divine, St. Patrick's.
The glorious Sistine.
Ornate spirals.   Massive gothic pillars.   Jeweled windows.
Glowing candles.
Gurudwaras in Birmingham.
　　　Langar.   Endless saag and makhi rotis.
Shinto shrines in Japan.
Delicate cherry blossoms floating to
　　　carpet the garden, the pond of gold fish.
Guan Yin temples in classical old China.
Flowing rivers past Hindu temples
　　　on the banks of the Ganges.
Vishnu. Ram. Shiva. Krishna. Kali Mata.
Saraswati. Sai Baba. Ganesh.   Laxmi.
Hanuman. Brahma. Durga.
Jewish synagogues. Shalom. Mazal tov. Yom Kippur.
Rosh Hashana.
Moslem temples.   As-Saalam-Alaikum.   Wa-Alaikum Saalam.
The Prophet Mohammed.   Friday night call to worship.
Russian Orthodox Churches.
Coptics.   The Baha'i.
A church of tin in the Kitengela.
Goats and sheep welcome.
Cows at the door, tafadhali.
Maasai economy beckons me.
Looking for god everywhere but myself.
Forgetting the way.

A gorgeous shaman priestess hidden
  at a forest shrine in Paik Du San.
Her black hair flowing.   Pure almond eyes.
Wearing a dazzling white silk robe,
  embroidered richly in red and gold.
Her attendants and nuns adoring her.
Tigers watching at the wooden gate.
Eternal. Lost. Forever.

XVIII

The man at his deathside,
Reflected on his life.
Where had he gone wrong?
How could he rewind?
How could he change?
Was it too late?
Bedridden, sick, riddled with disease,
He wasn't sure.

Mr. Raju Kapila quit.
The shastras, vedas, shabads,
    Artis, Krishna, Ram, Sita, Laxman.
Crap. A load of shit.
Why should he play the fool?
Turning to Canada,
    he lost himself.

If we stop to think about religion seriously, such will evade us.
If we don't take care, we will slowly, but surely destroy
        Ourselves on a lusty diet of defeat and misery, until
        We annihilate ourselves utterly by our own design;
Creating for ourselves the very coffin of our death and ceremony.
Hoping; yet, alive.

Beauty of my soul within, arise.
Take hold of my nature, create,
        breathe, see me in you.
A sequence of time and space.
I am the way, the truth and the light.
No one can come to the Father,
        But by me.
What did this mean?
How did it work?
Universality of God
Is only absolute.
His way is everlasting, sure.

To be in His Grace, a moment.
Speechless. Fine.   Ok.

So, Mr. Kapila took
    a teacher's license in Toronto,
    and began.
Gee whiz; kids are cute.
Always tomorrow.
Always today.
A third grader must somehow turn nine.
Their hopes and ideas were so fresh.
History, math, geography, reading, art.
Love.
No, he would not let them down.
He would show them the way.
He knew that skill; school.
In this way, he was free of guilt;
That his faith was too shallow for the real stuff;
    the true miracle and magic.
God has never existed;
He is always here.
Eternal.   Timeless.   Formless.
Real.
He saw God in every inch of his classroom;
    In the Italian kid, Irish, Chinese, Korean, Jewish, Punjabi,
    Turkish, Jordanian, Iranian, Gujarati, Pakistani, Kenyan,
    Serbian, Russian, Mexican, Nigerian, Guatemalan.
Where in the world was He not?
At which end did He fail to reach?
No where. No end.
And so, very kind Mr. Kapila
Continued Hanuman Chalisa on Oak Street;
    and was fine.
Rice and daal ok.
Once in a while a cheese pizza.
And his two daughters married
    Indian boys from New Jersey.
Everyone a doctor.

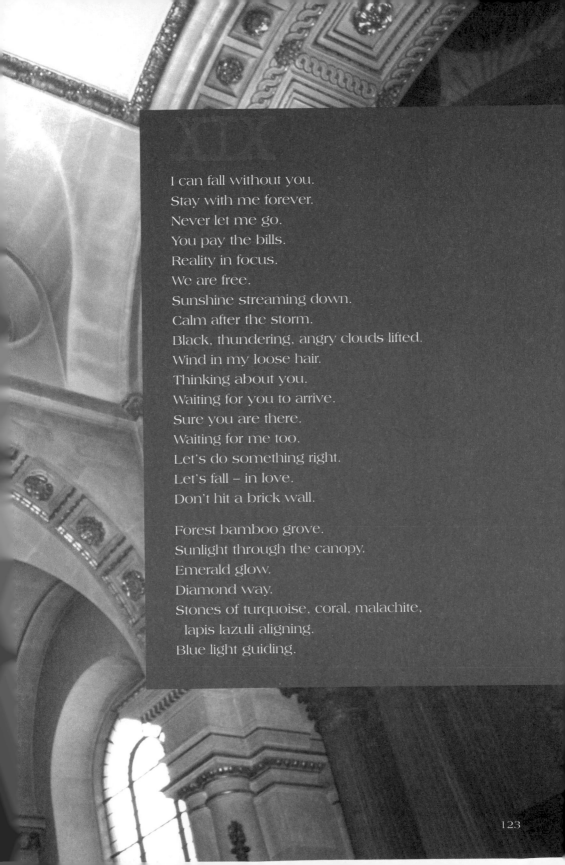

XIX

I can fall without you.
Stay with me forever.
Never let me go.
You pay the bills.
Reality in focus.
We are free.
Sunshine streaming down.
Calm after the storm.
Black, thundering, angry clouds lifted.
Wind in my loose hair.
Thinking about you.
Waiting for you to arrive.
Sure you are there.
Waiting for me too.
Let's do something right.
Let's fall – in love.
Don't hit a brick wall.

Forest bamboo grove.
Sunlight through the canopy.
Emerald glow.
Diamond way.
Stones of turquoise, coral, malachite,
  lapis lazuli aligning.
Blue light guiding.

XXI

Suicidal ways.
Darkened days.
Mother, why are you crying?
Sister, stop weeping.
Brother, your anger, hatred, is too great.
Child, you are lost.
Father, you are gone.
To deliver children only to
    mutilate them with hatred.
There is no way; no guide.
Forward darkened days surround me.
I can't see, and am lost.
What can I do?
To where shall I go?
How can I follow?
Who can show the way?
None but me.
In dangerous pursuit of ego, desire, rage.
Destruction galore.
Trees felling.
Polluting, belching factories.
Ludicrous presumptions.
Error ways.
Protecting my defenses, I eagerly wait.
A miracle will arise.
I know it. I am sure.
Here and now.
Always and eternal.
Miracles. Magic. Myself.
A thirst for right.
A quest for poetry.
Release. Freedom.

XXII

Heavy tree, burdened with massive,
    bushy, leafy branches.   Yellow flowers.
Solid trunk.   Roots extending.
Giving me its air.
Working tirelessly for my benefit.
Love.   Forgiveness.   Can I recognize this miracle?
God's grace?
My Mother, my Earth.
Silence is the greatest praise.

Having completely ruined his life at 58,
The man really had to stop and think.
Divorce, separation, lawsuit, bankruptcy.
Absolute loss.
So many faults, errors, mistakes.

The leopard watched with great sorrow
    the ruin of his jungle.
The machines that consumed and
    destroyed his home.
His beloved ngumo felled mercilessly.
The misery of endless economy.

To choreograph a dance of a thousand
    pliés, arabesque, chassés.
Pink, white, lavender, grey, blue, green,
Purple.   Black.
The painter recognized god eternally.
The flower, woman, fruit.
The land; himself.

XXIII.

Give humility a chance.
If all is silent, what is left
    is God's great beauty.
Spiritual guidance protect me;
    I am not afraid.
Facing evil.
Truth. Myself.
Feelings of anger arise from gross
    negativity.
Waves of ego, sorrow, shame, regret.
Peace to my brother and sister.
Peace to my most beloved and
    respected parents.
Joy to the Earth.
Love all around.
Praying intently on the Divine.
Contemplating His ideal, virtue, way.

White billowing clouds.
Crystal blue sky.
Green, fresh earth; dew, rains, sun,
    breeze;
Radiating glow.   Peace.

The subway rumbled past the church.
Inside, the people were praying, singing,
    weeping.

XXIV

My sister's wedding.
White dress parading.
A jewel.
My mother protect me.
My father to guide me.
Show me the way.
That I stand right.
Do my best. Forward.
The old priest wept in sorrow for man.
At his death, surely the temple would be
crushed.
Man –corrupted, evil, stupid.

I'm going to wear my Father's robe.
I'm going to put it on, and speak, write,
    And tell you about it.
The robe is of fine black cloth; a collar of
    crimson velvet and gold brocade.
A little short for me, I wear it fine; ok.
It suits.

Retelling this ancient vibration.
No siren call.
No false prophet.
No mind. Truth. All.
Comfort me in this time of hell.
Demon raging gravity.
What the outcome will be –
    no one knows.
No one dare consider.
Ruin, misery, death, loss.
A feverish, all consuming – love.
When I look in your eyes, I see me.
To capture time.

XXV

A wood carver in Tanzania.
Makonde.
Ebony, mahogany, ivory,
    camphor, teak.
Creating fantastic shapes of the surreal.
In the end he threw them all into the ocean,
    and watched his work and labor float away.

The shamba boy earned himself a
    scholarship to Harvard,
    and eventually became the
    lead environmental officer for Colorado.
Indigenous ways are best for god-healing.
Sacrificing vanity, ego, retail.
Suppressing mad-insane desire.
Lust. Greed.
Deaf to your mother's tears.
Gun in hand; ready to shoot.
Desperate – yet, alive.

XXVI

Suddenly she says something to break the silence.
It worked briefly.
The magic, truly, was over.
After lunch, good bye.
Sayonara.
See you when I'm around.
I'll send the check.

Days and ways of shifting sand.
Time passing.
This is not an age of recognizable humanity.

It was nice touching her.
Calming, reassuring to feel
    Her against my skin.
Love, kindness, warmth, desire.
Not irritating.
Not grating.
Not offensive.
Just, nice.
Solidly with God.
Word unspoken.
Truth revealed.
With each turn of the wheel.
Qualities dissolving and arising.
One more elegantly dressed Ph.D,
Working for the UN.
Set to save the planet.
Mercedes sports car.
Designer eye wear.
Gucci scarf.
Rolex watch.

Remedy for action.

No time to lose.

Only waste.

Misery driving compassion.

Compassion driving mercy.

Continuing.

Trying. Losing. Gaining.
Tomorrow.

Afraid to show my true colors.

Cautious about myself.

Unsure. Confused.

Making errors and mistakes,
again.

XXVII

Motherhood – devoted, honest, pure.
Making sure your children are first.
Seeing to their welfare.
Or, needing them around.   Maybe it's a joke.
Or, satisfying primal urge.
Or, a pure mistake, a pain in the ass.
Or, satanic evil.   Demonic loss.

Two girls sitting at a Thai restaurant
    outside the UN.
Discussing their project, research, thesis.
Vegetarians.
Funny how their favorite author was Jane Austen.
Bored.   Lonely.   Stupid.

My mother's delicious bananas.
Always fresh; carefully chosen, with love.

Expressions of God, overwhelm me.
Excite me.   Deceive me.
Intelligent man; written word.
Effervescent charm and passion.
If the church bells can still ring, I'll be ok.
Throw away integrity, skill, confidence.
It doesn't matter.
If we drag it through the mud;
    It was never ours anyway.

XXVIII

I love you lord, with all my heart.
To worship you, o, my lord, rejoice.
Be glad in him, for he is the way,
 the Truth and the light.
Send them to school to learn the rules.
Don't mind the bill.
The quality of repetition.
Why am I still doing this?

Let's go to war.
Guns, battles, destruction, pain,
 misery, hatred, mutilations, incarcerations.
My death. My self.

XXIX

The old forgotten books, finally,
   had to be thrown out.
"The Lutheran Hymnal."
"The Bible in Greek."
"The Book of Common Worship."
"The Eternal Vedas in Translation."
"Essays on Theology."
"A History of Quaker Meetings."
"Latin Phrases Expressing Love for God."
"Good News for Modern Man."
Their time had gone.   They were useless.

Humiliating our mother.
Raping her. Gouging her eyes out.
Condemning her to slavery.
Abuse, pain, suffering, fornication,
   irreversible, non-retainable, ever-increasing,
   non-organic waste and loss.
The immediate prospect of disaster.

XXX

An overweight child of 8, at a
  skating rink with her father.
His wife is an artist at the Catskill's hotel.
Renting skates. Gliding round. Hungry for lunch.
Getting fat. Getting angry.

A family of four at a Korean owned Japanese restaurant.
Sharing the tepanyaki table. Sister, brother, mother, father.
Using chopsticks. Eating sushi.
The girl is excited. The younger boy is unsure.
Mother quiet, watching. Dad paying the bill.

Meeting Julie at the airport;
    Returning from South Africa.
Mother's Day tomorrow.
Her kid shopping – candy covered chocolates
      with a colored plastic toy cap.
She had left for a week to attend the
    conference.

Who can write the laws on political
    crimes?
The International Court?
Jurisdiction?
Proof? Merit? Integrity?
Fairness? Justice? Righteousness?
Equality?
To understand the disease,
    is to approach the cure.
To say I am, is hope for the future.
A little honesty may go a long way.
This journey of life continuing along.

'You have made many films in your career.
Who has made more films, you or your
    husband?'
Aiyeshwarya, with a lateral head nod –
    'Same.   Maybe my husband.'

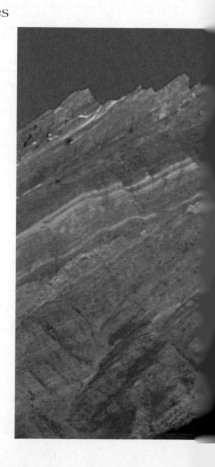

She lied on TV.

To make a family, one must look out;
    One must look in,
    To build the body of –
    Christ, Allah, Krishna, Buddha,
    Myself.
Morality changing, shifting, passing.
Still, we must stop, reflect, reason, consider.
Meditate.
A mother continually praying for her children
    to keep their senses.
A father carrying on, silently, in grief.
Indeed, the wages of sin are truly death.
No one listening.
Everything awry.   Wrong.   Of bastards.
Demons, witches, wolves, dogs, bats.

XXXI

She was overcome of fantasy and obsession.
Lust, vanity, absurd desire.
Her mirror could not contain her grief.
Exploding with passion, she breathed.
Again.   Otra vez.

SHREE MAHADEV

145

XXXII

A very capable son.
A blessing from God.
In His mercy and grace, God,
   who is our Heavenly Father,
   almighty power over all the heavens and the earth,
   again bestowed His mighty love.
Great compassion became born.
Again and again and again.
Everlasting. Fully engaging.
   Perfect, holy, decent, good.
Healthy seed.
Full hair; broad smile; good appetite;
   Respectful; well-mannered, humble,
   sincere, cautious, right.

IN MEMORY OF
FRANCIS ERNEST JACKSON A.R.A
BORN 1872 — DIED 1945
PAINTER LITHOGRAPHER TEACHER
THE PIETA PANELLING & ALTAR OF THIS
CHAPEL WERE GIVEN BY HIS PUPILS & FRIENDS

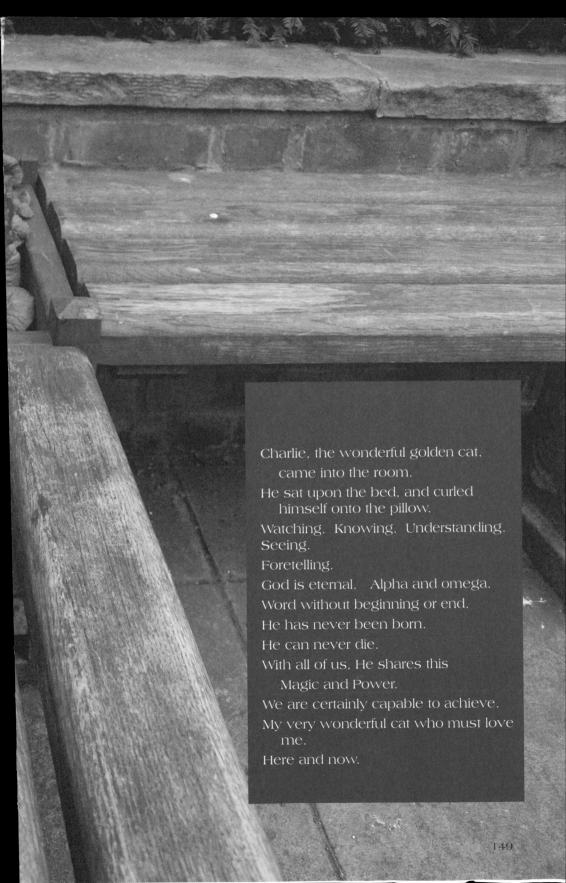

Charlie, the wonderful golden cat,
    came into the room.
He sat upon the bed, and curled
    himself onto the pillow.
Watching. Knowing. Understanding.
Seeing.
Foretelling.
God is eternal. Alpha and omega.
Word without beginning or end.
He has never been born.
He can never die.
With all of us, He shares this
    Magic and Power.
We are certainly capable to achieve.
My very wonderful cat who must love
    me.
Here and now.

XXXIV

Her sex, astounding beauty,
    was truly, surely, madly profound.
Let someone else do the work.
Pass the buck.
Duck. Renege. Hide. Shame.
How quickly can you lose yourself
    in sexual fantasy? Greed? Stupidity?
Lust? Sin? Loss?
A moment.   Fraction.   Totality.
A life led by bitterness, hate, disappointment,
    fraud, mistakes, regret; is no life at all.

The man sat opposite his daughter.
They were at a diner.
He had to tell her he was leaving for good.
His daughter looked at him, her eyes
    intensely full of hatred, anger and disgust.
The pain, truly, was unbearable.
He said his final and last good-bye;
    Turned, and walked out.
She was left alone; her food untouched.
Out of school, 16 and weeping, she was pregnant.
O fucking shit.

XXXV

How can peace occur?
Giraffe in the early morning sun.   Tall.
Browsing among the acacia thorn.
Peering over the tree tops.
Lunging forward.   Silent.
A cross between a camel and a leopard.
Neck and body adorned with reticulated spots.
Looking like a walking brick wall.
Four stilt-like legs.   Two stubby horns.
A snowy white egret on his back
was cleaning insects.
In the new-day sun.
Impala racing; spiral horns dancing.
A hairy water-buck stood still.
His gaze transfixed upon the horizon.
A cool, light breeze tossed the leaves and branches.
It doesn't matter what you eat;
Meat, vegetables, grass, insects, trees,
berries, nuts, lizards, snakes.
We are all loved by God.
We are all enveloped by:
Grace, wisdom, kindness, forgiveness, generosity.
Beauty.
Each one of us can unlock and
share this wonderful jewel,
this priceless gem.
Acts of mercy.
Acts of God.

How? Where? Why?
Think. It's not illegal, yet.
A group of fifty black and white zebras passing.
No two the same.
Each different.
Unique; special.
Their plush black tails swishing
across their plump black and white bums.
Like a song.   A symphony.   A play.
Birds calling;
doves, larks, hoopoes, swallows, boubous.
A conference of birds.
'Which way is the kingdom of God?
How can we express our joy?
How will we know his messenger?
Where do we find His forgiveness?
Grace? Kindness?'
On and on they called, pined, mourned, sang, praised.
'When will we see His face?'

At the salt lick.
40 zebra, 3 kongoni, 4 giraffe.
Strength in numbers.
The giraffe splayed his two front legs.
He reached down his long neck to
taste the delicious earth.
He was young. Maybe four years.
God's paradise revealed.

XXXVI

Repentant of my world.
Aware of my actions.
Keen to follow God's pure and holy way.
Keep his word.   A lamp unto my feet.
Bible, Koran, Torah, Prajnaparamita Sutra,
    Dhamapada, Vedas, Aurobindo, The Mother,
    Shankara, Sri Sri Granth Sahib, Sri Vasistha, Sri Vyasa,
    Bhagvad Gita, I-Ching, Surya Namaskar.
Myself.   Me. I.
How have I found love?
In which way am I discovered?
Through you; through me.
A young, tall successful man
    adoring his pretty, sweet wife.
Maybe this time it can work.
This powerful journey.
The right way.
Signs working ok.
A love so wonderful, it was real.
More a lie, not believing.
A story of two swans, loyal in love;
    Cranes, herons, ducks, stuck together.
Always following each other, in flight.

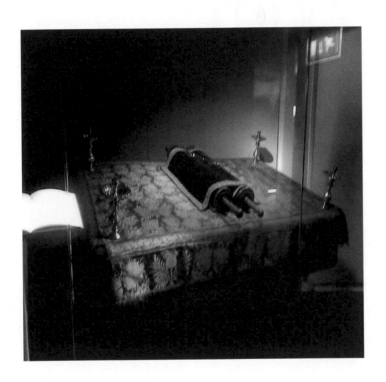

XXXVII

'You will need shoes when you get to the city.'
The sunlight was filtering through
    the cracks of the mud hut walls.
Flies were buzzing.
She quietly fished out
    her last 10 cent coin
    from the rusty tin can; and,
    gave it to her son.
He left without another word,
    silently promising to return soon.
He was sure a job lay ahead, waiting.
The corporate executive considered.
His third wife, five kids.
It was all so confusing.
It had all gone so terribly wrong.
How? Why?
His secretary buzzed.
5 minutes until his next meeting.
Then, a flight.
Hundreds of emails.
Phone calls in every direction.

XXXVIII

Islamic holy consumerism.

It's kosher; it's ok.

And then, we so easily lose our way.

Only to be guided back by our All-Forgiving,

    Eternal Father; loving us mightily;

    Caring for us constantly.   Begin.

He cries; weeps.

Begin now, and change.

Time will never stop.

Events will continue to arise.

Opportunity continuous.

Just open your eyes.

He murmurs.

He breathes.

Touching our hearts infinitely.

Seducing us to His way.
No pain; no regret; no fear.
Just pleasure. Joy. Bliss. Peace.
Love. J'taime. Amour.
I love you.
I need you.
I want you.
I am forever yours.
Completely. Endlessly.
Against all time and manner,
I am always near you to follow and join together;
    Again.
There is something funny about Ramadhan;
    You just become nocturnal.
Joseph, Yusuf, Yusuq*. I am.

* Mrs. Joan Yoo-sook Paik Sikand, Esq.